Faith 301:
The Results of Self-Love

Atlanta, Ga

ISBN: 9781944901301

Copyright © 2025 by Speaking Freedom LLC
All rights reserved.
No portion of this book may be reproduced without written permission from the publisher or author, except as permitted by U.S. copyright law.

Book Cover by: Kaci Winslow

Publisher Website: speakingfreedom.org

Other Website Information: SpeakingfreedomTV.org, edu-freedom.org

Publisher Address: 75 Washington St. #1177, Fairburn, GA 30213

Speaking Freedom Books' Disclaimers

Welcome to Faith 301: The Results of Self-Love

We thank you for your purchase and look forward to helping you grow in all areas of your life.

We hope that you find all the information needed for your growth. God bless. Please listen to all disclaimers provided.

If you are currently under a physician's care, please maintain that relationship. This audiobook is not intended to stop your current treatment plan. If you need physician's care, please seek out medical attention.

All results are based on the individual's ability to adapt and adjust to any given environment or situation. We are not responsible for your results. The life-enhancement coaches at

Speaking Freedom provide information to help you grow.

You are responsible for maintaining that growth, taking on and applying the information to your individual life, as necessary.

This book was written by Speaking Freedom Books, Concept by Kaci (Winslow) Myers. May contain and explain explicit content.

Please use parental discretion. For best results, you will need an open mind, the ability to research, and a balanced lifestyle.

Section 1: Setting Your Intentions

During the course of this book, the goal is for you to have your intention set on what you desire to manifest from this book. To do that, we want you to set your intentions, meaning get your mind on something that's your true heart's desire.

The intention of this book is "the best version of yourself." Imagine yourself as your most fulfilled self. While reading this book, we want you to set your intentions on learning, accepting, and understanding the best version of yourself.

That means seeing your wildest dreams by envisioning yourself in those situations, meetings, and other things that you would like to manifest. There are going to be questions posed within each section to help you quiz, understand, and grow yourself more from the previous section.

Each question is to help you think about and even write down your answers so that you can get to a deeper level of faith within your life and your faith walk.

Journal Thoughts

What do you imagine your best self to be?

If you could be anything in the world or have any type of success, what type of success would complete you and make you feel fulfilled?

If you never had to work again and you could do anything for the rest of your life, what would that
be? (without worry about getting paid money)

What do you believe your gift and calling is?

How would you like to see it manifested to its fullest potential?

Section 2: Self-Love and Acceptance

Going into this section, let's discuss a very important topic to consider when you begin to examine, love, and accept yourself, it's a phrase I call "Christian denial."

Christian denial is when people decide to use their faith in Christ to magically erase all of their problems. Meaning instead of addressing the things that bother them, their concerns, their past, and their childhood traumas, they just use Jesus as a magic eraser. Then say that they are no longer the person that they used to be.

The denial is found in not addressing who you used to be so that you can heal, grow, and learn from those things to ensure you never fall back into old behavior patterns. This is important when it comes to self-love and self-acceptance because a lot of people tend to deny parts of themselves, their past that they are ashamed of, parts that help to tell their story, and their testimony in the future.

Christian denial is an extremist mindset where you can't even own up to your own actions and accept your responsibilities or accountability. When you are unable to be accountable, responsible, and really examine yourself, you are unable to really grow to your fullest potential and really accept your where and why God has placed you in that position, then who your need to become.

It's important because this is what causes people to have depression and to have things that they cannot get over because they're not willing to address. So instead of healing, they put a band-aid on it and use that band-aid, which can be church, money, or material possessions. That band-aid makes the hurt rot because it never gets the exposure, healing time, and breathing room needed to help that person move on and grow in that area.

When that person gets that time to grow and comes out of Christian denial, then they can address every single core issue, trauma, hurt, and pain that they've ever experienced and grow by accepting their entire life journey as it is. It is only when you accept your entire life's journey that you will truly grow, that you will be able to embrace who you are and where your future is destined to take you. Addressing Christian denial is really about being real with yourself.

The more real you can be with yourself, the more real you can be with the universe and God, and the more you can assess what your purpose is and how to grow within yourself and for yourself on purpose. You also have to take care of your physical body. Now, as you begin to address the things that you've gone through in the past, it may lead you to address the concerns of your physical being.

Whether you are dealing with or struggling with physical health problems, mental problems, or spiritual problems, those things, especially physical and mental problems, will begin to manifest in your spiritual world. Your physical health problems can manifest because of unhealed emotions and distress that you feel. When you are real with yourself, able to see beyond Christian denial or anything that limits accountability, responsibility, or healing from your past experiences, you can grow, accept, and embrace where you've come from.

As you begin to take care of your physical body, that also includes taking care of your mental and emotional needs. Most of our physical struggles come from an emotional imbalance which causes a chemical imbalance that makes the natural processes of our body shift.

Addressing your health concerns is a very important part of selflove and acceptance because if you are not physically at your best, you will not be able to give your best. The goal is to be able to be healthy physically so that you are capable of doing more, be more, and enjoy your life more.

You must work on your physical and spiritual wellbeing. Ladies and Gentlemen, you really need to get checkups, even if its daunting, most heart disease and other preventable illnesses would have better outcomes if detected early.

If you are sleeping around or sexually active, please go get HIV and STD tests. Ensure that you are physically healthy and that you are not carrying around any disease that you may not know has manifested in your body. Work on your spiritual well-being. What do you feed yourself spiritually? How do you think spiritually?

What things have helped shape you so that you can stay on course in your spiritual life? What things help you balance out who you are as a person? When you get to talking about the spiritual sections of life, you do need to have some relationship with the universe, a higher power, or God.

If you are a person who does not believe in God or have a religious preference, what I would suggest for you on your spiritual journey is to be more at peace and one with yourself. Get connected deeper to your soul so that you can feel and be guided based on your true heart's desires. I would prefer and would like for you to try to learn more about the spiritual world so that you can be more informed about good spiritual balance.

You can be religious, but it's great to know the truth behind the religion that you follow. When I say learn the truth behind the religion that you follow, that means do history research and lessons on the culture that you have decided to follow. If you are not of that heritage or culture, you should also get spiritual knowledge on the spiritual practices of your ancestors.

If you are indigenous to this land, then you should get all the information that you can find about those indigenous to this land. If you are Hispanic or Spanish, you should get all the history about Spain and being Hispanic or whatever your Hispanic background is. If you are Native American, you should get all the information related to your ancestors and all the Native American tradition of spiritual practices and more that you can find related to whatever tribe your grandparents, great-grandparents, and ancestors were from.

If you are from Africa, I would like for you to seek out all the spiritual knowledge about what they practice in Africa. What I don't want to continue to happen is that we take on Christianity as a blanket statement and we don't know the heritage or the background of our ancestral bloodline. So then we are not able to live up to where our people come from and use that to fuel the message of love that Jesus and religion are supposed to be carrying.

You also need to make sure that you evaluate your state of mind. There are times when you may need to seek therapy. Every therapist normally has a therapist or someone that they can talk to because they take on people's problems, issues, and dilemmas all day.

It is perfectly healthy to seek help if you need therapeutic conversation. If you go and seek counseling, there are different types of counselors that you can seek. There are different types of life coaches you can seek.

You need someone who's going to feed you with positive information, someone who can hear you, understand you, and help you solve issues. And not just by, however, the book told them to do it, but by someone who can help you walk out and apply things to your life based on your issues, your dilemmas, and the solutions that would be helpful for you specifically.

You have to evaluate the state of your mind.

How do you think? What are your thinking patterns? Not only what are your thinking patterns, but what are the behavior patterns and perspectives that cause you to think that way? When you begin to think about your thought patterns and your behavior patterns, your thought patterns come from your perspective. Your thought patterns can be judged and evaluated by your perspective, what you post on social media, the things you say, the way you view things, how you act, the way you project your thoughts on others, the way you understand others, your compassion, etc. When your thought patterns are a certain way, they will begin to reflect in your behavior patterns.

Now a very honest person, their thought patterns and their behavior patterns will align. However, a person that is not the most honest will have one set of thought patterns and then you will see a noticeable difference in their behavior patterns. When you come around people or when people come around you, they expect to see in actions what you've said, in your perspective, what narrative you entertain, and objective you have.

As you begin to evaluate that for yourself and begin to view your own thought patterns, perspective, and how that changes, enhances or alters your behavior patterns, then you will see and be able to further evaluate the state of your mind and what type of therapy you need. Now, therapy comes in different shapes and forms. You may need a business coach, a life coach, or a clinical therapist. You may need a therapist who also can get you to a psychiatrist so that you can get medicines if needed on a temporary basis.

I want you to understand you are uniquely you.
That means you have to be real with yourself. Everything that you've gone through, everything that you face, everything that can play back in your mind at a later time. Even if it's not something that concerns you now or

is not a part of your life right now, it can come back up later if you don't deal with it.

Honestly, not dealing with it is the issue. The goal is to help you be able to deal with anything that you face from this point forward. So if there are things that you have buried, if there are things that were previously unaddressed, as you begin to heal yourself, take care of yourself more, grow, and encounter new things in life, there are situations that may come that will trigger old thinking. You have to be mindful of things that will trigger old patterns of behavior, trigger thoughts, or areas of healing that you may not have properly addressed.

These steps will help you address those things in a way that allows you to heal. The goal overall is for every time you address a new area of healing, a new area of perspective, a new area to level up in, a new layer of enhancement, you should be able to play back these things that you're learning here and use those developed skills over and over again, as things begin to progress in your life.

As things happen, there should be no new challenge that you do not know how to face, because you've understood the process of learning yourself, accepting yourself, and being completely 100% honest with yourself and with your creator.

Again, at the end of the day, you are uniquely YOU. You have to be real with yourself. You have to be real with your beliefs and why you believe that way.

You have to be real about your trauma. You have to be real to heal the things that have made you feel any type of way at any time. So if something has altered your mind, your perspective, or your behavior, those things in time will be addressed for healing, so that those things don't affect you again.

As you begin to heal, you will begin to see how your mind and your heart opens up, how you become very free despite what you're facing. So you have to begin to observe your struggles and understand how your struggles made you stronger, better, and wiser. If you're in denial about those things, you can't grow in those areas.

If you start addressing issues within, then every day that you realize that you need more healing, you will go within yourself and pick apart where the core issue stems from.

Evaluate these things and ask yourself tough questions. What struggle did this stem from? This triggered mentality, reaction, and thinking pattern, where did it come from?

In the case where it's not a triggered behavior or triggered thinking pattern and you've already altered your life in such a way that nurtures the hurt versus nurturing the healing, you have to take it back within yourself and say, okay, where did this start?

How did I get here? And what can I do to make the appropriate changes so that I don't remain here? Sometimes this can go into having to let people go, removing yourself from certain situations, environments, and establishments. You may have to switch jobs.

Now, don't quit your job until you get a new job, but you may have to make certain changes that help to heal you. Because in the process of healing your mind, you heal your soul. If you can clear up your mental anguish, if you can heal and work on your thought patterns, then you will automatically heal within your behavior patterns.

Your behavior is what it is because of your life experiences and how that has changed your perspective, your thought process, and how you've decided to deal with things that remind you of that situation. All of these things won't necessarily be bad things. Some things are just not in the best interest of where you see your life going, but it's not necessarily bad for everybody.

As you begin to become more purpose-minded, begin to fulfill your soul purpose and align with your calling, through your gifts, skills, and everything that has created you to be you. Understand that the things that do not align with where you desire to go will begin to naturally fall away. As you begin to observe how your struggles have made you stronger, you will come out of the survival mode mentality and you will begin to create new ways of living that will help you thrive beyond the survival senses. There are certain things that you needed to go through to help strengthen your mental, physical, and spiritual endurance that made you stronger, better, and wiser.

When you begin to break down the things that you've gone through and how they've impacted you, you will begin to find value in each lesson gained from experiences. As you evaluate and acknowledge how you got to where you are, you will see growth. Those things play into the type of people you like, the type of men or women you date, the types of environments you're willing to put yourself in moving forward, and where you see yourself going long-term. How do your goals play into where you see yourself going long term?

Everything that is within you is what you need to fulfill you. Every challenge that you face, your attitude, your personality, everything has been intricately put together, placed into your life, and into your path to help you for every step of your journey. So, accepting, embracing, and then collectively learning from every situation is key.

Find where you've become stronger. Note to yourself how you were before you faced the circumstances that changed you and how it helped you grow after you faced it. How will you move forward with the lesson that you're learning currently from how that old circumstance evolved you?

A blessing is a lesson when you can evolve while learning from what you're going through. Learn about yourself and the people around you.

A lot of dealing with yourself is accepting and acknowledging where you've been and how you've grown. Growth is also related to those you surround yourself with. If you place people that are in denial around you, then you will begin to make excuses for yourself and be in denial. Either you become more like the person that you're around, or they become more like you.

If you place yourself around liars, then you are more likely to stretch the truth to obtain whatever results you're going after. But this is about your true self. This is about the person that you cannot deny, the person that you cannot run from, the person that you cannot just turn off.

There are things that people would call your "demons," and things that people would say torment you. The things that people have told you are wrong about you, that need to be fixed or changed for you to progress, aren't always as bad as people project. The actuality is you were created for your faith to be made whole for your purpose.

The things that make your faith whole are the things that you were designed to accomplish on your journey and purpose. Your gift and calling may be completely different than anything that anybody else has faced. You may have certain things about your personality, your characteristics, your sexuality, or aspects about you that are supposed to be different. You are called to be YOU.

You are an individual. You are not called to be just like anybody else. Everybody is trying to be a standard of what others should be, missing out on who we were called to be, often unable to build the kingdom at hand.

God's kingdom is the universe according to love, self-acceptance, and being compassionate to others. To be compassionate to others, we have to first be compassionate to ourselves to help others take better care of themselves spiritually, mentally and accepting the true version of who they really are, through life experiences and circumstances.

Some people are sheltered and unsheltered, who still have crazy life experiences. If you can be sheltered and have a crazy life experience or you can be unsheltered and still have a crazy life experience, then whatever the universe created for your path, your journey, for growth, maturity, physically, or any area is designed for you specifically. Just think about it, somebody else can go through the same exact thing and have a different outcome, different perspective, or a different view. They can have a different understanding of self-acceptance.

As you begin to accept yourself, then you see where other people tried to change you to be more like what was acceptable to them based on how they were raised and what they believe. But you have to figure out what is best for you.

What is the best thing for you, based on your calling? Your calling is going to be based on your gifts, your natural abilities, and the things that you can't help but do.

That means it may tie into your attitude. Although there may be instances where you shouldn't have an attitude, there are also instances where that God-given attitude will protect you as you move forward.

Gaining tough skin has a way of protecting you. Even being vulnerable can be for your protection, but keep in mind that some people's hearts are cold. When a heart turns cold, they often have no sense of compassion because they were not shown compassion.

There are two sides of the spectrum. There are people that were not shown compassion, that become very compassionate because they know how it feels to be handled without compassion. Then there are people that have received no compassion, so they will show no compassion to others. Often, the thought process for having a lack of compassion and vulnerability, or the lack of being themselves is because they feel it's gotten them further.

Honestly, it may get you further, for instance in a system, but within it will leave you drained and unfulfilled. The goal is to be fulfilled within our purpose, soul, mind, and body so that we can give those that we love and ourselves the best of us.

If we aren't a hundred percent, then we can't give our families a hundred percent, we sure can't give God a hundred percent and we can't give into the environment that we're creating for ourselves at a hundred percent. Consider how being raised different or changing one experience could change everything in your life.

There are some things that you regret that have helped you to become your best yet. If you are honest with yourself, the best version of you has come from some of the most trying times of your life. The one thing that we don't realize is that if we change one thing, we could change the whole course of everything. So if most things in your life are going right, but you go back to change something, you could change things for the worse, just like it could be for the better.

What I want you to do is focus on how the experiences that you've had thus far help your future. How does it prepare you for the next opportunity, circumstance, challenge, and ability to overcome? You have to find your greatness through your testimony, truth, and the experiences in life that helped you create this version of you.

This version of you helps you create the best next version of you. A lot of times you will hear, "You can't live and be who you were created to be while being who you used to be." When the actuality is, who you used to be is how you became who you are currently and builds who you were meant to be.

Who you are meant to be in the future is a combination of learning every single lesson that has been presented to you through the struggles and circumstances that life has presented as a part of your path and journey. Consider your old goals. Can you still honor those? Consider the things that you thought you wanted before and consider if they're still complementary to where you're going. When thinking about where you desire to be or any of those old goals can they be fulfilled in the things that you were called and created to do now?

There are some things that you may have thought about doing, like going into politics. If life took you a different way, would it mean that you were not meant to be in politics? It just means that your political stance may come from a different aspect than what it would normally have if you had gone the politician route.

A lot of times we have to realize that for something new to happen, we have to go a different way. We can't keep going the same exact way that everybody is gone, that is not working, and still think we can go that way to make it work. Unless you're coming with new information, a new mindset, or a new way to establish yourself you will continue to recycle the same experiences, challenges, and struggles. You have to apply the lessons of life to see change. With everything you've encountered in your journey, the lessons that you get aren't going to be the lessons that somebody else receives. Nobody else is doing or experiencing the same thing that you are doing and experiencing.

There are things purposed for you specifically. Be able to sit down and think about the things that you wish you would have known before. Then evaluate how you can apply what you can learn moving forward. If you find yourself thinking, I wish I would have known that or I wish I could have done that differently. Start to reshape your mind about challenges that you face every single day and apply the lessons that will turn your "I wish list" into an "I did list."

If you are faced with the same type of dilemma that you faced before, how do you make the changes necessary so that you don't end up with the same exact outcome again? Learning the true you is equal to learning how to navigate your soul in this human body, existence, and experience. We are souls on earth living out this human existence.

The more you learn the depths of your soul and how to navigate in this body, the better you will be able to navigate the future of where you're going with your family and friends. It is very essential that you establish your foundation on the lessons from your past.

Love on yourself, no matter what you've been through. It doesn't matter if you are confused about your sexuality, attitude, the way you were raised, or who you are in society today; begin to use that confusion to build yourself up. Also never question yourself based on somebody else's opinion.

It's easy to get caught up in somebody else's opinion and start to change for approval, but you know what you've overcome and how you became who you are. Use that to your advantage.

Journal Thoughts

How can you accept yourself better?

Name five things that you struggle with accepting about yourself and list ways that you can work on being more accepting of those things.

If you are religious and you struggle with sexuality, molestation, or any type of addiction related to your sexuality or porn, learn from it. If you've ever struggled with drugs or any type of addiction where your mind isn't sober, learn from it.

How did you get into the things that you are into?

What is it that you are trying to bury within you?

What are you running from that makes you want to seek to cover it up or change your personality?

Do you do things to drown out your feelings with things that leave you unfulfilled?

When the sex dries up, when the liquor wears off, when the drugs run their course, you still have to live, deal with, and face yourself before anybody else.

The goal with this particular section is to help you face yourself and face anything that comes your way with confidence that you have won this way before, knowing you've overcome every struggle that you face, and you were built for the life that you are creating.

Section 3: Pursuing Your Purpose

When you pursue your purpose, you have to know that it is deeper than religion.

Religion can stifle your purpose if you are not willing to live your specific purpose out fully. There are things that you were purposed to do that you will not be able to find in the Bible or in whatever religious text that you are reading. There are a lot of things that have changed from when the Bible and The Quran were written, as well as other Sacred Texts.

A religious undertone of your purpose may not be able to be found in the Bible because times, people, and circumstances have changed greatly. As we evolve, who, what, and how we understand the concept of the universe and God has to grow and evolve also. God is not stuck in the past; God is in the now. There are very standard principles of living that religion can help you understand when you are introduced to God as the creator of the universe.

However, when you really get down to your purpose, you have to seek God directly. There are no limitations in the kingdom of God or in the universally manifested creation we call earth. You have to find your purpose so that you can pursue your calling. Remember there are no limitations.

If you've read the first 2 books in the faith series, Spiritual Human Behavior or The Unknown Power of a New Believer, then you will know that the key to finding your purpose is getting more acquainted with yourself, your gifts, and understanding how to put everything into practice.

Figure out what would you like to accomplish that's bigger than yourself, or that's bigger than simply self-gain. What would you like to do?

How do you want to impact the world in a way that will help you to succeed in your life, without selfish motives? Remember It's okay to make money using your talents and skills, as long as you keep your principles.

This section helps you remove all of the status quo attributes of success to figure out what would fulfill your purpose. When you can answer the following questions, you will have a better understanding of how to structure your life.

*Answer with Journal Thoughts

What is it that you see yourself doing for the rest of your life that's beyond you?

What did you need when you were young? What did you see yourself in need of growing up?

What type of mentors would you have liked?

What type of things would you have liked to be different or to see change, etc?

When you begin to see or recognize the things that you needed growing up, it may spark the nature of your purpose because those are the things that you should help build up in other people. The things that you lack should not be the things that you attack.

What do you do naturally? There are some things that you've been taught to do second nature, but there are some things that you do naturally. Think about it, some people can just sing naturally. They don't have to take a class. They don't need to do vocal lessons or training. They just open their mouth and it's like the heavens.

There are some people who are good with marketing, don't need a class. They are simply good with marketing.

There are some people that are just good with numbers. They don't need to go to school or a class. You put an equation in front of them and they do it naturally. All these things that I've stated are natural abilities, but when you think about gifts, you think about something more spiritual.

Everybody has a spiritual purpose, and everybody has spiritual gifts of some sort. Spiritual gifts do not have to be something spooky. It could just be your natural ability. You may naturally and spiritually be an administrative type of person.

You may naturally and spiritually be a prayer warrior. You may naturally have the ability to help people mentally from a spiritual place. Whatever your natural ability is, it's definitely connected to your purpose, and you should feel encouraged to use that to do something bigger than yourself.

Self-gain and making money are okay; however, do not get caught up in making money. Make sure you use that money to help push your purpose, to help influence and encourage others to be better. You should be able to use your gift, your purpose, and your skill to make money. But if you're going to make money, use that money to help further and flourish your calling, to help those around you, and to do good in the earth. Do not be so consumed with yourself that you cannot see that you can impact the world with your natural abilities.

What bigger purpose will you dedicate your life to?

This is different for everyone. If you're a person who didn't have great parental guidance, then your purpose may be intertwined with being a good parent. When you can be a good parent who raises well-balanced children, your children grow up to be great in society, and then you've already impacted the world in a way that nobody else can.

When you've given the world well-rounded adults who want to better the world and who want to play their part in the bigger picture, you create change. What will you dedicate your life to? How will that help progress the world around you for yourself, your children, and their children?

The goal of Speaking Freedom as a whole is to help the world grow in a more love based purposeful dynamic, that helps other people grow the world in a more purpose-filled dynamic that becomes a continuous cycle.

If you've been helped, then you become a blessing to help someone else, then they become a blessing to help someone else in another continuous cycle beyond anything that you could think or imagine.

What has worked for you in your life and favor so far?

There is a saying that your gift makes room for you but there is also a saying that wherever God guides you he will provide for you. So, if the universe is guiding you in a direction, then you will see the doors of heaven favor that direction. You will see provision; things begin to go your way and working out to encourage you to continue down this path.

The path is different for everyone and this is why it's important to know yourself. You must know where you've been so that you can begin to realize where you are called to go according to your specific purpose based on your skills, gifts, talents, ability, mindset, willingness, determination, and ambition.

All of these things play into your bigger picture along with what has worked in your favor. Always remember some things don't work out for everybody. Pursuing your purpose is using the things that you learned about yourself, especially from the previous books so that you can see what has worked.

What has favor attached to it?

What are you doing that every time you do it it works without question?

What are you doing every time you decide to go this way, offer this thing, or do certain things that works?

There are situations that you can place yourself in that will work for you because it's you. It's the grace, favor, and provision of your life as needed according to your purpose. When you are figuring out the parameters and getting into your purpose, things will work for you.

It might get difficult at times, but it's going to work. It might bring circumstances that challenges your level of comfort but grows you and it will work. The goal is to figure out your purposeful niche. What is the thing that you do without question that will work? That every time you do it, it works.

I'm not telling you to go sell drugs or commit a crime because it worked for you. I'm not telling you to use drugs, drink alcohol, or go strip because it works for you. I'm not telling you to do anything that you do not believe is truly connected to your purpose because money is involved. Favor and money are not the same thing.

Now there are things that money can buy that can seem like favor but then there are things that will not be in your favor regardless. There is no amount of money you can get in certain doors. There are things that being a hustler cannot get you, but the favor of your purpose will gain you access to. You should begin to fine tune your purpose, really take heed to what works, then use what works to work your purpose.

Take note of these things:
1) Your patterns.
2) The things that do not work as much as what works.
3) Who is around when it works?
4) Whom God removes when it doesn't work, and God is trying to get you back on the

right path. 5) How have the things that you've gone through changed you?

6)   The behaviors that you need to continue to work on.

7)   The things that are in alignment with who you are and where you're going. Knowing your patterns can save your life because you have to know yourself better than anybody else. The better you know yourself when things challenge you, the better you will know how to respond.

Who is around during your biggest accomplishments? Knowing your patterns will help you but knowing who you win with will also help you. Think about it, if you know your patterns but you bring people around that throw your patterns off, your way of thinking off, your compassion off, your gift off, and you become stagnant because the wrong people surround you.

If you are not able to fully embrace everything that comes with your purpose or you don't want to walk your path, check yourself and then the people around you.

Reshape your thinking and set your focus to the positive results. A lot of pursuing your purpose is denying yourself the things that you're forcing and accepting what comes in natural alignment. Accept what comes with grace and favor. Also accept where your purpose leads you. Your purpose is going to take you down a path. It may be a familiar path or an unfamiliar path at times.

The more you know about your gift and calling, the better you can nurture it. For myself, because I realized that I have dreams and that I see people and I understand people and I am in tune with people on a deeper level it helped encourage me when I began to realize that I like psychology.

It helped to encourage me as I began to realize that I like banking and finance but not in a way that I wanted to pursue that totally and solely. The more I realized how much human behavior played a part in the world the more I wanted to learn what my soul was attracted toward. This connected me to my purpose of helping people grow. When I began to see positive results, like most people, it helped influence me to continue that path.

When you become addicted to positive results that are connected to purpose you become unstoppable. As you pursue your purpose the confidence that you have from seeing God's favor becomes addictive and the very thing that keeps you going.

When self-doubt hits and everything looks like it's a mess, your wins connected to your purpose will keep you ignited. It will keep you moving forward in a way that you will never want to look back. Make a list of the things that you see yourself doing that's attached to a purpose, something that's bigger than yourself and will impact the world in a huge way.

Normally, it's something that you always think about, that's already inside of you and although it may seem difficult you can see yourself doing it. Actualize the things that have worked for you thus far and then make the adjustments. If you see that you've been doing x, y, and z for the last two or three years and nothing with x, y, and z is working, then it's time to go back to a, b, and c. This is the key to not disregarding your goals because you were not able to do it the way that you thought it could be done.

There are times when you have to adjust the plan to reach your goal based on purpose. You should never throw away your whole goal because one thing went wrong. You make the adjustment.

Again, there are no mistakes. This is a live-action experiment of life on a journey that you are figuring out as you go. Nobody knows what they're doing until they've done it, and they've learned from it.

Some people can help guide you, but your life is for you. You need people who support your purpose. You need people who complement your goals.

You need the people that will help feed your soul when it gets weary. Not people that will drain you but people that will help you grow within your purpose as you pursue it daily. That pursuit of purpose will fuel you to continue the journey.

Journal Thoughts

What would you like to do to impact the world?

How would you do it?
(Make an elaborate plan. If you want to travel the world and change the world that way, then say exactly what you would like to travel the world to do. This is one of the things that I would like for you to write down and make note of so that you can, in your mind, begin to figure out how those things could happen for you.)

Figure out what you need to do and what adjustments need to be made as you pursue the purpose that you believe that you're blessed with. We've already been uncovering how to walk in our purpose so, pursuing your purpose is not giving up on yourself and what you know.

Don't give up on the lessons that you've learned. Don't give up on the trials that you have to go through to shape how you will move forward in your purpose.

*Questions asked within the chapter can be answered along with these questions.

Section 4: Creating The Vision in Meditative Prayer.

In Faith 201, we discussed creating a vision board, getting supplies, and the creative process of vision boarding, but that's just the beginning of creating your vision in meditative prayer. To really embrace where your life is headed, where you desire to go, and where your goals are leading you, you have to stay in a constant meditative state.

That doesn't mean you can't go anywhere, do anything, or think about anything else. Being in a constant meditative state is just being open to always hearing from God (The Universe) to speak to your heart and soul; This comes in many different shapes, forms, and fashions.

Being in meditative prayer means always being in communication with God and always taking the initiative to make the next step in moving forward with grace. So that means sometimes you need to go and you need to look at your vision board that you've created or the one that you will create potentially, eventually. When you're looking at that vision board, pray to God within yourself.

When I say pray to yourself, that means say a prayer that's either under your breath, in your head, or praying out loud to God instead. Ask the creator of The Universe, God, how do I reach this? How do I accomplish these things? What is it that I need to know to carry out the vision board that I've created for my life? It is very, very important that you concentrate and spend a lot of time reviewing the vision that you've created for your life.

Throughout the course of this journey, you're going to constantly go back and check to see if you are accomplishing the goals that you've set out. You'll need to constantly review your vision board if you do not keep it in front of you so that you can have a constant reminder of the things that are set before you. Seeing the goals that you would like to accomplish so that you can always be mindful of how what you're doing today makes way for the vision of your tomorrow.

During your life, you will have continuous opportunities to develop your soul, adding to where you see yourself going, and making the adjustments to your vision as needed.

Honestly, there may be times when you need to go to your vision board to either add or remove something to update and fine-tune the vision. There are things from the original stages of creating the vision board, that I thought meant one thing and it turned out to be something totally different.

If I didn't stay in meditative prayer about the vision created and what leads to that, then I would have been thrown off by trying to force what I didn't fully understand in the beginning.

The way that you see things may not be the way that God designed it. Personally, I placed things on my vision board in a way that in my mind, it's understandable regardless if you're reading it top to bottom, right to left or left to right, so that it tells a story.

The story that you see when you look at your vision board may be a different scenario and synopsis of what God meant when he placed it in my heart. For us to continue strongly down this path, we have to keep the meditative mind of prayer. We have to constantly be aware of where we're going, and where we've been and ask God (the creator of the universe) how to proceed so that we don't have any stumbles, we don't trip, we don't fall, but that we make great decisions and that we align purposefully with the vision that we've created for our manifested reality.

I do have to warn you, if you are creating a vision board for the first time, you don't just have to do a vision board on a cardboard or a dry-erase board and make a collage. There are several different ways that you can begin to manifest. Some people burn candles, some burn incense, and some burn sage, all of these are used to set the atmosphere by helping to cleanse, meditate, and recreate the energy that you will manifest. Some of these practices can be done with lists of things that you're believing for.

These practices are done with hopes and desires in mind. There is a method called a faith jar. This is done by getting a jar, cleaning it out of course used or buying a mason jar from the store, writing down things that you believe God for or things that you would like to happen in your life, then placing each in the jar. None of these have to have a date on them and don't have to have an order, but you're going to put all of these things in a jar.

You can also fill the jar up with accomplishments throughout the year, so you can look back at the end of the year and see all that you accomplished.

It's at your discretion to tell or show anybody the things that you put in the jar, your vision boards, or your prayers. The things that you are creating for your purpose are meant to be personal development tools and these personal development tools will begin to change your life.

If you're doing a vision board, using candles, and writing down what you're intentionally manifesting, a faith jar, writing a vision for your life so you can see it, or jotting down your dreams you'll see your life change. If you are a person who is a visionary, has dreams, sees things vividly, or gets insight from God, then the more you write down things to know where you believe that God, the Holy Spirit, (The Universe) is taking you, the more you will begin to see your life change.

There is a disclaimer that you need to know when doing a vision board or when trying to manifest in any manner at all. As you begin to write down things and believe God (The

Universe) to manifest those things, you need to know that your life may go a slight bit haywire. I'm letting you know this because you are requesting God and The Universe to align you with the vision for your life and align the things that are supposed to be in the vision of your life.

That means the people, places, things, character development moments, attributes, and everything that is associated with your purpose must come together in total alignment for growth and manifestation of your purpose. This also means that everything mentioned must be in alignment separately for things to work.

If any element outside of yourself is out of alignment, then things can be delayed until something or someone else comes into alignment with God's plan. If the plan is not working God will also redirect you!

When you start to believe for the vision on your board or other tool, you'll notice the need for changes in your behavior, thought process, and the alignment necessary for you to manifest everything. Trust God even if your life gets turned upside down, don't panic, it's a part of the process.

Don't make challenges along the way become your excuse or the reason that you don't try to do a vision board or manifest your dreams. It is my responsibility to make you aware of what you're going to endure. Remember people will fall away, then people will come together; things might fall away, and other things will come together. You will go places, see things, do things, and experience things that will play into your growth and overall development.

You have to be ready for what you're asking for. There are things you have to go through that are going to prepare you for the vision that you see for yourself in your life. They may not always be easy things.

There are effects when you begin to attract the things that you desire in your life. Some changes will take place. There will be an imbalance at times so you can gain balance at other times.

Create an intentional life. If you know that you want to manifest all of these things, then don't just wait for the universe to make your life topsy-turvy or get it out of order. You can begin to make the adjustments on your end where you see fit. If you know adjustments need to be made for the things that you want to manifest to be manifested, don't hesitate.

The goal is to work towards your prayer. Be willing to work on and towards everything that you've prayed for, the things that you're believing for, where you see your life going, and so on. Take time to embrace and enjoy your process.

Let me be the first to remind you that your process will not be what everybody else's process is. You may have to endure a season of being alone. If you have children, a spouse, or both you may still need a season of separation in order to reach your full potential.

That does not mean that you're going to have to divorce your spouse or get rid of your kids. What that means is that while parenting, in the midst of being a partner to your life partner, you may have to take more time to sit aside to figure out what God (The Universe) is doing through you. You might need to pray for understanding for your family to face challenges along your path. Prepare them as you prepare yourself to fulfill your purposeful path.

Everybody has a path and a purpose. Everybody isn't willing to seek out their purpose. Out of the people who seek their path, they will walk in purpose. Some will know their purpose and will not follow the path.

A bigger purpose has a different path. A smaller purpose has a different path and likely fewer moving parts. It doesn't matter what you're called to do. You have an individual path for your life that you have to walk out.

It may involve and include the people that you love. If you're married, your spouse is a part of your purpose unless your spouse doesn't align with your purpose, makes you stagnant, or hinders you from fulfilling your purpose.

Then there are some cases where someone might marry a person who is not purposeful for their life because purpose considered. That can lead you to separate or divorce. We are not teaching separation or divorce.

However, we also know that there are times when you may have to go your separate ways so that you can both pursue your purpose. You need to be with somebody that's in alignment with your purpose. That doesn't mean that you get along all the time or somebody that's going to sugarcoat what you're doing to make you feel better. You need people who refuse to play into your fears or hinder your spirituality, your sexuality, your mentality, or your physical capabilities.

You need people that are purposeful. The people that are purposeful for you will challenge you to be better, seek more, and do more, then they're going to walk with you through it. Purpose to purpose. The people that are for you will be complementary to your life and purpose.

Embrace your individual process. What worked for your mother, father, or whoever else, even if they have a similar calling, may not work for you or be in alignment with your purpose. No matter how similar a person's purpose can be, it will not be the same because you are not the same.

I want you to embrace your individual course. You may have kids before somebody else or have kids out of wedlock.

There is nothing that says that you're wrong if you live your life different than somebody else, other than religious judgment. We want to dispel religious judgment so that you can feel purposeful to pursue your dreams according to how your soul has aligned your life. The nature of fulfillment starts with spoken word, then written word.

As you begin to speak your words and write your words, you manifest your words. When you do your meditative prayer while reviewing the things that you desire and actions that will help you be in perfect alignment. Review exactly what your vision says that you should accomplish and how you should accomplish it. You will see your life begin to change.

Sometimes you won't notice until you actually see a shift, the progress and the adjustments that you've made alongside with the universe aligning your life. So the more you stay open to a meditative approach of accomplishing your goals, visions and dreams, you will be removed from the hustle and bustle of chasing money, people and things that don't add value to your soul worth.

As you begin to add value to your soul's worth, some things won't be as attractive or alluring. You will begin to see yourself develop. You will begin to see the change and note the growth. Now this could happen in two to three months or two to three years. The bigger your vision, the bigger your purpose, the longer the path.

Make sure that you understand that when you're creating your vision board, your vision board may not look like the next person's vision board. Your faith jar may not look like the next person's faith jar. And this is the only reason that we suggest that you don't share your vision board or you don't share the things that you place in your faith jar.

We don't want you to try to compare how your vision is different than the next person's vision. We don't want you to try to compare how you may be designed to do this way and somebody else is designed to do it a different way. Your vision board will look the way your mind works.

So if you ever want to know how your mind works, create a vision board, create a faith jar, and everything that you see no matter how junky your vision board is. Your vision board may have a ton of things and somebody else's vision board may not have a low. Some may have a lot of words; others may have more pictures than words or yours may have more words than pictures. Somebody else may have a balance of pictures and words and may say different things from person to person, but you have to find what's right and what's true for you.

It's okay for each vision board and vision to be different.

Journal Thoughts

How can you begin to manifest the things that you've placed on your vision board?

What can you do to work towards what you feel in your heart and soul?

How can you begin to align your mind with the grind that it takes to get to what you desire to manifest?

Whether it's manifesting relationships, travel destination places, a career, or whatever you desire, it starts in your mind with the meditative prayer to help you stay aligned.

Now, it is very important that you are reminded, do not try to rush through the process that has been created for you. Everybody's process is different. Your process will not be the same as somebody else's process.

Proper preparation and opportunity is a success. Allow your process to be completed based on what your sole purpose is and don't be ashamed of it.

Section 5: Seeking Personal Spiritual Clarity Daily

Now that you understand meditative prayer, the importance of knowing where you want to go, and reviewing those things on a regular basis. It is also important to seek clarity and daily guidance to keep yourself encouraged.

Try to wake up every day and pray every day. Then review your vision boards, go over your goals, and the things that you have planned long-term, and create a schedule that will help you work towards your long-term outlook.

When reviewing your vision board and goals, get so familiar with it that as things play out in real-time, you recognize how everything is working together. Think about your dreams.

If you have vivid dreams that you can remember, begin to write those dreams down so that when things happen in life, if it aligns with a dream that you've had, you have a point of reference to go back to. You can look at your note and say, " I had this dream, this happened that has flourished or manifested in my life and this correlates with that dream in a certain way."

Also, begin to jot down important thoughts. With social media, we tend to place a lot of our thoughts online, but make sure you have everything written down for yourself just in case your account or a particular platform is shut down.

There is nothing wrong with sharing online if the visionary thoughts that you have and see for yourself manifesting in the future could benefit a bigger picture outside of you. Create points of reference for yourself through journaling so that you can go back and you can know what is happening and impacting your journey.

When you keep a journal, your ability to reflect becomes better and you can say, "I dreamed of this, I saw this, or I experienced that." Think about your goals and the actions necessary to align with the things that you desire to manifest. If you are doing and working towards the things that get you to where you want to be, then it's easy for God (The Universe) to send things your way according to your path to keep you encouraged.

Here are some examples of how favor and provision can guide you.

If your purposeful path is designed a certain way and you follow the alignment, good things happen simply because you followed the direction that resonated with your soul. The favor and provision serve as guidance, especially when you don't compromise your morals, values, and your integrity.

Let me give you another example of how your path is made through provision and favor as a guide.

If by chance you decide to do your own thing and you get out of the perfect alignment, there will still be things that happen in your favor. However, those things will lead you and guide you back to your perfect alignment. No matter where you are, there will always be a guiding light that will keep you enroute to your destination of manifestation.

Shape your mind to think positively when everything goes right. Say this sentence out loud: "This is the provision for the purpose of my life and this alignment is allowing that provision to happen."

Your goals are designed to help you understand your soul better. This is the reason for the meditative prayer and seeking God (The Universe) for the gathering of our goals, purpose and what we do with our life? Guidance is available if you are open to moving outside of your comfort zone. What's inside of you needs to come to life creatively and unapologetically.

If you never go into your heart (soul) and mind (spiritual capacity) to understand yourself better, then you will feel lost. You have to discover what your purpose is through understanding your talents, gifts, and things that you desire, and then learn how to use that to create a purposeful life. It is very important that you think about all the things necessary to reach your short-term goal and your ultimate purpose.

What are the steps? How do you prepare for that? It's like counting the cost to be the boss. Before you build a house or you work on any type of project that requires equipment, tools, or supplies, you have to assess what you will need, what challenges you may face so that you can properly prepare for any changes. This is the purpose of having spiritual clarity with daily meditative practices to get the guidance that you need to stay aligned with what you're desiring to happen.

Work what works. If you figure out something works great for you or if you get clarity about the route that you're taking and it works, continue to work that avenue. Continue to see what else falls in alignment within the path that you're on that allows you to work what has been working for you.

The things that you are called to do will be in alignment with your purpose and it will all flow without force. You won't have to have 10 things going 10 opposite directions. It will all flow based on your ability to love and embrace yourself, to commit fully to your goals, hopes and the purpose that God has placed in your heart.

Work what works. If you find something, a thought pattern, a mindset, or actions that work, Work That! If you connect with people who complement what you do, your purpose, and your goals then work those connections by having something to offer as well. Work What Works. This is not to create manipulation or for you to seek people to use by only working with what they have to offer while providing nothing. Everything should be a mutual exchange.

The goal is for you to get more in tune with who you are, so you can work what you have because everything that you need, you have. Even if you have to learn a little bit more or fine tune it, work what works without manipulation of anyone else. Enhance your craft where needed.

Find ways to learn more about what you're enthusiastic about. If there are things that you're passionate about, that other people do, have done, or experienced, connect with them to learn.

Remember other people have already done the legwork so that you can learn more in a shorter period of time, but you still need to reference check everything. If somebody has already done some of the work, then you can check for updated research so you're not doing double work and you can ensure that you are fully informed.

Your research may show you something different and take someone else's ideal further even before you hear their ideal. There have been many times that I've listened to books that took a thought pattern that I had a little bit further because it confirmed something that I was already thinking before listening to the book, and allows me to expand my thoughts further.

The more you feed your soul according to what you need to align your purpose with your lifestyle the more fulfilled you will be. Building your life around your purpose instead of building a purpose around a life, you have to gravitate to what's for you. You have to learn to enhance the things that you already see developed within yourself. You have to become your biggest cheerleader, your biggest support.

Figure out what would you do if nothing else worked if nobody came along to save you. Work what works. Figure out what your magic is. Find your niche, find your provision, create your own wave, and then ride that wave until it takes you to where you desire to be. Work what works!

You will definitely need continuous self-evaluations. You need to figure out what parts of the process is good for what you're doing and what parts of the process need to be refined or redefined. Go over your notes constantly.

Always look for ways to improve what you're doing, what you're working on, and who you're becoming. Always seek improvement. Always seek enhancement.

Always seek growth. Now that does not mean to always be looking for the next best thing or to become a destination addict saying, "I'll be happy when I get this and I'll be happy when I go here and this will work out when this happens." That is not what we're telling you to do. We're telling you, instructing you, and helping you to figure out what works according to your purpose.

Set reasonable goals, even if they're long-term goals that you can accomplish by putting in work. Allow alignment to help you pursue, obtain, and accomplish everything that you've set out to accomplish. Your process is Your process. We can get so caught up in someone else's accomplishments that we don't notice that their process has them connected to a different path, purpose, or something that may complement what we do, but it's not exactly what we do.

Purpose is not a competition. This is where the world comes together and helps each other to succeed, grow, show compassion, and show purposeful alignment.

So don't think that your process has to be like somebody else's process or if they get a little bit further, a little bit faster, that something is wrong with what you're doing. Focus on your focus. Focus on what works. Work what works for you!

Be purposeful, be mindful. Don't try to do what somebody else is doing if it's not for you because somebody else may be graced to do something you are not. Somebody else may have favor in what they're doing and then you try to do it and there's no grace or favor. Leaving you to feel bad, unfulfilled, and all these other things because you were trying to apply your purpose to somebody else's process or somebody else's process to your purpose.

Create the journey by walking out your purpose. The path of your purpose is created as you take every step of faith.

Capture tunnel vision. Get so focused on your vision, purpose, and goals that nothing else can distract your mind from what you're seeking to accomplish. If you seek to accomplish that thing and you work diligently at it, eventually you will begin to see your goals manifesting into reality. Sometimes it happens unconsciously because you may not always have your vision board present. You may not always have that faith jar right there.

You may be so caught up in manifesting that you don't have time to think, "I said that I wanted to do this and it's happening.

I said that I wanted to experience this. I'm manifesting the things that I said that I wanted to do. It's happening."

Actualize your goals by focusing so strongly that it becomes tunnel vision. You don't see anything else. All you see is the things that's relevant to your purpose and purposeful alignment.

As the relevancy and the purposeful alignment come together, you will begin to see the floodgates positively open on your life. The way you measure if you're going in the right direction is understanding that the right direction will begin to give you the right results.

I'm not going to tell you that during the course of going down the right direction, it won't feel like something is off. There are going to be things that are going to challenge you to see if you are going to continue on this route toward your purpose.
There are going to be things that will test you.

I am not saying that you have to struggle. You should not have to endure some extremely difficult challenge, but there will be things that happen as a part of your life that will test and challenge you. You may lose people to death or because you had to disconnect as you seek your purpose.

You may not go places and it may be because it's no longer valuable to the purpose and the soul alignment that you are seeking to obtain. Be blind to anything that is not purposeful.

Be blind to negativity that tries to drown out your purpose so that you don't pursue it.

The goal is to be the happiest, most fulfilled person that you could ever imagine being, for real. Not the facade of "happy.' Not the facade of this is what's going on.

Life will never be perfect based on what other people deem perfect or see as perfection, but it will be perfect for you because you're learning life lessons. You are enduring the things that were purposed for you to become the best version of yourself. So you're going to be seeking regularly to get clarity.

The more you seek clarity, the more you understand what's going on in your life, the easier it will be to face any challenge that comes your way. There will be things that you may struggle with at first that become a challenge that you overcome later.

When challenges come, what is going to hold you is the things that you know in your soul, the things that you've accepted and you've been able to learn how to use for growth.

Journal Questions

What can you do to help yourself gain more clarity day to day?

What things, people or places can you eliminate from your life, your mind, and your circle to help you have less negativity in your life?

Are there any people that make you doubt your purpose because they don't understand it?

Now, I'm not saying that you will have to cut these people off permanently, but there is a great portion of reaching manifestation that takes a little bit of separation so that you can elevate properly without distraction.

When you are walking in faith, one of your goals is to eliminate as many distractions as possible.

So your individual process has to be what you can sustain. And even if it gets difficult, knowing the vision makes it easy. Now you have to continue to work the plan, the process and allow the manifestation to happen naturally.

Remember, Work what WORKS.

Section 6: Developing Your Gifts and Talents

In previous books, we talked about talents and gifts, but let's take it a little further here. Developing your gifts and talents really is about practicing what you truly believe and knowing why you believe it so you can practice it.

The goal is to build comfort through practice, recognizing, receiving, and building up your confidence through developing your gift, talent, skills, and craft. Evaluate what environment your skill, gift, craft, or talent works best in. If you're an artist as a singer, songwriter, writer, painter, design artist, or any type of creative lane, then your artistry may be developed differently than someone who has a gift or craft or skill in prophecy or something that's along the lines of education.

You have to find where your gift works and it will make room for you so that you can build the comfort of using your gift without having to think about if you can or should use your gift. Everybody has different talents, different gifts, and different skills based on their specific individual purpose, the more you tap into those gifts, skills, talents, and crafts, the more you will begin to unlock and unfold your true purpose. What helps you feel comfortable using your gift? That will also feed into your purpose.

What environment does your gift work in? What environment are you able to practice your faith, talents, and skills in? Where does your craft work the best?

This entire book is designed to help you learn, get comfortable with, and accept yourself much more. Ask yourself, what setting would you like to be in vs what setting works? If those two are totally different, how can you find a happy medium for both?

There may be someone who needs church as a medium when introducing them to God.

Church may be a part of your gift development for your purpose and you may have a complimentary artistry that's needed for a church that allows you to impact people in a great way.

If that works for your gift and skill as a part of your purpose, then use that time in that place to grow yourself in your gift, skills, and to learn as much as possible. This helps build your confidence in ways needed to walk into your calling as you practice things that you are developing for the bigger picture that God (The Universe) planned for this connection.

If you are someone that does any kind of therapy, massage, emotional or relationship, then your environment to work in could be in an office setting or a social platform where you can feed people what they need therapeutically. If you are a massage therapist, of course, you can't use your gift online on a social media site because you cannot massage through social media. You have to learn what environment works best for you.

If you're a therapist of the mind, then you may be able to do more than a person who is a physical therapist or a massage therapist because those are hands-on. So your environment is going to be specific for your purpose, tasks, and alignment so that your gifts flow seamlessly in that particular environment. You have to practice what you're saying you're believing, what you believe plays into the things you do and practice regularly.

Divine presence is sometimes a part of the gift and the lesson that leads to the blessing. Define your talents and gifts in various aspects.

That means if you have a gift, use it in different ways so that you learn your gift fully. We want to help you. It's like if you're a singer, then you want to learn the vocal range of your gift and talent so that you can master your craft.

It's the same way with any other gift, skill, or craft. You have to develop so that you can learn the range of your gift. Let's say that you have the gift of prophecy and your prophetic gift is based solely on relationships and interactions, but someone comes to you and wants you to interact as a medium with the no longer living.

If your prophetic gift is not as a medium, then it would be a disservice to yourself and to the person who's asking for you to try to act like you have the skills of a medium if that's not your gift. A Spiritual Medium is a person able to communicate with the deceased.

You have to define what your gift entails, the shortlist and the long list. What is the broadness of your gift and how you can use it? What is the minimum of your gift and how it can be used? Because at different times, you will need different settings for your gift.

It's like a computer or anything that you have to change the settings on. If you have a camera that has different settings for the pictures that you may want to take or the functions of the camera, the different settings are for different things. So you may have a different setting than the next person.

Somebody may be able to write, sing, act, and do a whole list of things, but your gift and talent may be more precise, more powerful, and more focused. This is something you wouldn't know until you start to practice the development of your craft, gift(s), skill(s), and talent(s).

What enforces the focus of your gift? What helps you focus better when it comes to aligning with your gift and calling? Meditate of course, but is there anything else that encourages your focus and full attention?

We know you're going to pray. We know you're going to look at your vision boards, but what internally helps you focus more? What works within your gift? We talked about what works in your faith. We talked about what works in manifesting.

We talked about what works in creating the vision board and how to critique and add to that. But what works with your gift? Focus on the things that lead to your vision regarding perfecting your gift and your craft. Sometimes you may have to go places and when you're going there, you may go thinking one thing, but you may end up using your gift where you least expected it.

The goal is to figure out how your gift uses you. If your gift is a part of your soul, then how does that gift use your human body to flourish? Flourish as much as possible within your gift specifically. What platform works best for you? What is your desired outcome for your gifts? Is there something that you see yourself doing as this gifted person? What could you see yourself doing for the world? As you begin to develop your gifts, talents, and skills, you will become more aware of how you can use those things to impact the world in a big way.

Define your talent and how you will use it with your gift for your purpose. So you may have a spiritual gift, but you may have a different talent that if combined with your spiritual gift will ignite into something much larger. Your purpose, if you are a writer and you have a spiritual gift that goes along with your writing, combines your spiritual gift of administration, prophecy, the gift of speaking in tongues, or being able to heal with touch.

If those things align with your talent(s), skill(s), and ability, or if you can align your talent with your gift, it will help you develop your purpose that much more. Your gift may be your talent. Your talent may be your craft. Your craft may be your skill. If you have understood yourself for a long period, then those things may go hand in hand.

When you understand who you are and what your purpose for, the more you can feed that purpose through development, knowledge, and wisdom in your growth.

Be sure to determine how you will use your gifts and talents. I'm saying to determine it, but it's really about alignment and how it helps you become more of who you're called to be. It's a natural gift if you can do it without thought. You can enhance your natural gift through knowledge, education, and practice.

If you can do things that help you get closer to using your gift in a more natural, fluent, and broad way to help more people, then that will help you fulfill your purpose and be able to shine your light further.

Focus on purposeful interactions so that you can have the opportunity to really exercise your talent(s), gift(s), and skill(s) to develop them. The development comes with practice.

Practice comes with interaction and close encounters.

If you're reading this book, I pray you begin to walk into your purpose, develop your calling, then accept and move in your purpose as it comes naturally to you. Do what works based on what your purpose is. Plan your steps. Adjust the plan as you begin to step in alignment with what you know that you are supposed to do from within then determine how you'll continue to move forward. Have a plan of action. Have a plan of development.

For some, you won't be able to plan. Some things take action and you adjust as you begin to continue in that action. But you have to develop what you're supposed to do by practice.

It's like being an intern. Intern your gifts with onthe-job experience. Get experience with yourself, your gifts, and your purpose.

Take some time to do the things that you are called to do. That will either do one or two things. It will validate and certify your calling within to give you confidence or it will show you exactly what you're not supposed to be doing.

There are some things that you may feel like you're not talented enough to do or that you're not called to do, but you have to endure your developmental process to know what's for you vs what's just a good idea. Some things are good ideas that won't lead you closer to your purpose. There are some things that you do well that may help complement your purpose and your gift but are not the main focus that you should be taken up with.

Learn what's for you through developing what's within you.

Journal Thoughts

How can you develop your gift more?

How can you practice your talent?

How can you prove yourself to yourself regarding your gift(s), your talent(s), your skill(s), and your craft?

Begin to work that within everything that you do so that you can become more purposeful, so that your faith can be built up in confidence about what you've been called to earth for. When you can base your life on knowing what you believe, practicing what you believe, and believing what you know. Then you will know what you believe.

Section 7: Balancing It All Out

This is the section where we learn how to balance out everything that we've learned thus far with spiritual and physical balance along with balancing life. What would you consider to be spiritual balance? Allow this question to ponder your mind as you begin to develop and understand what balance should be when it comes to spirituality. We want you to get a clear understanding of the spiritual world and the natural world, and then find balance within yourself.

You have to consider who you are as a soul on a spiritual level and what you were sent to the earth for. So as you begin to consider all the things that we've talked about up until this point, who do you consider yourself to be as a soul? Where do you find soul alignment in your mind versus what you believed before? How do you balance out your physical with your spiritual?

This will be different for everybody because your spiritual nature may not be the same as someone else's. Remember you may have a different heritage and background in spiritual culture outside of what you've been told about the Bible, religion, and Jesus.

Honestly, I believe it would be in your best interest to understand the background of your heritage as well as whatever religious beliefs you have. According to your soul, you may discover that you have a different purpose than what's been laid out before you.

Consider who you are as a soul and how that changes on a spiritual level based on what you know about faith as of now. Why do you believe you were sent here on earth? It ties into your purpose and what you will do for the world as well as with your spiritual gifts. Now, all of that is a part of who you have been developed to be since you were a small child.

All of these things go together even though it may not seem obvious at first, all of these things are for
the betterment of your alignment. Your understanding of alignment can balance your natural world with the spiritual components of who you are.

Understand the mind and God's Love as a light worker. If you believe that you're called to change the world to do better and to spread light and love, then you need to understand the mindset of God as a person who is graced to help other people.

A light worker is somebody who believes that they are called to share the light and love of God (The Universe). You will also begin to shed old things. As you get a clear understanding of spiritual and natural balance and how to produce the reality that you need, you will begin to shed old hurt, old energies, and things that no longer fit into your purpose.

Some things are not meant for where your life is headed based on the goals that you have set, your purpose, your gift, your skills, the vision, and your meditative prayer that will help guide you through this course of life that you're in.

Take in the earth and the world around you. Really begin to remove your blinders, begin to see the earth for what it is. Take a day, go outside, observe the land.

Wherever you live, there is something unique about the place. Observe the butterflies and the animals that you encounter. Observe everything around you and see how those things begin to guide you.

The power of how you believe is your power in manifesting. So being able to balance your natural with your supernatural and spiritual will help you be able to manifest things from the spiritual world and God (The Universe) into your physical reality. Your task is to understand the balance that you are creating from within based on your purpose.

Thank you for your purchase. Please check out our
other books.

Spiritual Human Behavior
Faith 101
Faith 201
Faith 401
The Unknown Power
It's My Time

www.ingramcontent.com/pod-product-compliance
Lightning Source LLC
Chambersburg PA
CBHW070443090526
44586CB00046B/1964